CONTENTS

No table of contents entries found.

No table of contents entries found.

ACKNOWLEDGEMENTS

My thanks go to my wonderful wife, Lista, a source of strength and encouragement, and to my wonderful daughters, Mbwemi and Esther. Without your patience I would never have done this. Dave Clemo and Mark "Spud" Kennedy also get kudos for encouraging me to self-publish. My appreciation goes to Kenny and Sylvia Young, for proofreading and for their continued friendship. Mention should be made of the late Dr David Allen, who taught me Church History, made me laugh and ran a poetry competition that I won, and Dr John Andrews, who said, "If you feel called to write, write SOMETHING!". I finally got around to it.

My greatest thanks go to Almighty God, His Son, Jesus Christ, and His Holy Spirit.

Great Galumphing Granny

Like a peal of rumbling thunder, Like a lancing lightning strike,
Great Galumphing Granny comes bounding into sight.
Carrying heavy shopping like a lighter load,
Onward, ever onward,
Galumphing down the road.

She has lunched on marvellous Marmite, with butter, if you please,
And Granny, glorious Granny, galumphs beneath the trees.
See her wondrous bounding gait, her gargantuan gangling stride,
If you see her coming,
Show respect and stand aside.

Cause her no distraction, stand not in her way,
For this is Great Galumphing Granny and this now is her day.
You cannot halt her progress, or ever slow her down,
Granny gamely goes ahead,
Galumphing into town.

She's more than just a legend, she's as real as she can be,
If you have the patience, then you will plainly see,
Her classic, checkered, carpet coat, her fluffy padded boots,
And the favour that she always shows,
To those who wear smart suits.

As she fades into the distance, and she galumphs now passing by,
You might feel some regret, a tear come to your eye,
But do not dally in dismay, or wonder where to turn,
For you can be so ever sure,
Galumphing Granny will return.

First Things First

First things first and last things last,
The way that it should be.
But why are others always first,
And the last is always me?

<u>Name Dropping</u>

I have great respect for Roger McGough,
So I'd never, ever rip him off,
And I'll tell you that I truly admire,
The work of Benjamin Zephaniah.
I would quote you, if I can,
The genius of Spike Milligan,
But for now I think I'll stop,
And think of other names to drop.

Always Allitterate

Agitate an awkward apple,
Tease tubby tins of tea,
Dampen Derek's dark delights,
Make merry mocking me.
Run races writing raucous rants,
While wildly wondering why,
Brilliant buzzing bumble bees,
Start stinging sunny skies.

Burn brightly baking bulbous bread,
For funders freely found,
Carve creepers, cautious, carefully,
Seek Steven's solid sound.
Hail holy heathens helpfully,
Neatly knocking nuns,
Get gleeful goblins gardening,
Pondering perfect puns.

Zip zoo zone zombie xylophones,
Gamble great green gates,
And, whatever else you do,
Always alliterate.

Take 5

Take 5 and take it easy,
Take 6 and have one more,
7 now is greedy and 8 is just a bore.
9 is totally tempting fate,
And so we won't go there,
Going back may be an answer,
For that we must prepare.

4 is where you're feeling it,
And you're stressed out by 3,
Take 2 is just another take,
1? Well, wait and see.
I think that we should stick at 5,
By far the safest place,
I'll leave it now for you to choose,
I think I've made my case.

Sadly Missed

Were you ever He Man, Master of the Universe?
Maybe you were Skeletor, or someone even worse.
Bravestarr had eyes of hawk and ears of wolf as well,
Speed of puma, also there, but what of sense of smell?
Did you cheer Inspector Gadget, with niece and dog, what's more,
Also see him blunder, yet defeating Dr Claw?

Ulysses 31 took Greek legend into space,
With his son and scanty crew and the gods upon his case.
Battle of the Planets was an earlier delight,
G-Force aboard the Phoenix, fighting the good fight.
Teenage Mutant Hero Turtles, not Ninja in UK,
Wheeled Warriors and Transformers always made my day.

Memories of childhood, from a simpler time,
Lacking PS4 and Xbox, its passing is a crime.
Wonders kept in mind alone, now rarely ever seen,
I wish that they would once again appear upon the screen.
To regain the sense of wonder that was each episode,
And every minute being in full escapist mode.
Maybe it's because of age, today's 'toons aren't as good,
Bring back all the classics, I really wish they would.

The Wondrous Tale of Grizzly Jack

Grizzly Jack, Grizzly Jack,
Brought down a tree with one big whack,
And dragged it to the railway track,
Which ran down to the sea and back,
He never again experienced lack,
The wondrous tale of Grizzly Jack.

<u>Complex Theology</u>

(A poem based on the theological positions of belief in the removal from the Earth of Christians, by God, before, during or after the "Great Tribulation. For more information, see, *The Book of Revelation* in *The Bible*)

Pre, post or mid, pre, post or mid,
You know, I'm really not sure,
Whether it will be pre, post or mid,
The snatching away of the pure.

I know that whether,
Pre, post or mid,
It will be like a thief in the night,
But will it be pre, post or mid,
I want to get it right.

Pre, post or mid, pre, post or mid,
It used to be so plain,
But now I've heard of pre, post or mid,
I'm having to think again.

I know there'll be troubles,
But pre post, or mid,
How much will I see?
And will it be painful, pre, post or mid,
And will it overcome me?

Pre, post or mid, pre, post or mid,
Now, I'm not saying I'm clever,
But I know that whether pre, post or mid,
I'll be with Jesus forever.

Reformed Theology

(Another theologically inspired piece, this time making reference to the medieval practice of buying "indulgences", or supposed relics of religious significance such as pieces of the cross, in order to shorten the time that would be spent in Purgatory. This was an annoyance to the reformer, Martin Luther, who had recently discovered the doctrine of salvation by faith alone. The original version of this poem won first prize in a poetry competition at Mattersey Hall Bible College, 2004/2005)

When the trumpet sounds and the Lord calls me home,
I'll be glad of the indulgence from the "donkey from Rome".
As we meet in the air and sweet praises sing,
I'll be ever so thankful for the coffer coin ring.

As I walk through the gates to the great Bema court,
And show to the Lord all the relics I've bought,
He'll be so pleased to see them and to know my true worth,
He'll be glad he released me from under the Earth.

When I think of the Battles,
The struggles with sin,
I'll say with some pride,
I bought my way in.

Mosh Pit

Heaving bodies, sweating mass,
Waves of effort,
Forth and back,
Music raging, flying hair,
Push further, faster,
If you dare.
Crazy surfers risk to ride,
The rising, flooding surging tide,
And divers dive,
Caught by the crowd,
Play it hard and play it loud,
I'll feel the bruises, and the pain,
But that's for later; GO AGAIN!

<u>Mythomane</u>

(Being one with a seemingly natural inclination to be untruthful or to dwell in fantasy land)

I'm Mythomane, I cannot lie,
No that isn't true,
You cannot rely on that,
As lying's all I do.

But is that true, or is it false?
You can only guess,
There will be no certainty,
Whatever I confess.

You could, forever, live in doubt,
Or take me at my word,
Or "hmm!", and, "ooh!", and, "umm!", and, "aah!",
Questioning what you heard.

I'm Mythomane, I do exist,
But with all I've said,
Are you even sure of that?
I'm messing with your head.

A Different Point of View

Wee Willie Winkie, running through the night,
Wearing just pyjamas, giving kids a fright.
Wee Willie Winkie makes old ladies jump,
Running, ever running, a half-naked Forrest Gump.

Wee Willie Winkie gets the wrong attention,
He appears on Crimewatch, with a special mention.
Wee Willie Winkie is portrayed as quite a fool,
By the various people who knew him when at school.

Wee Willie Winkie cannot understand,
The negative publicity is getting out of hand.
Wee Willie Winkie thinks it's not a crime,
To run about in nightwear telling folk the time.

Limericks

One of two college deans,
Always dined on baked beans,
The gas he would shift,
Passing wind in a lift,
Creating some terrible scenes.

There was a young man from Dundee,
Who thought that he was a bee,
He'd spend every hour,
Around a sunflower,
And only had pollen for tea.

An old woman eating an orange,
Tried and tried to rhyme "orange",
With all of her might,
She sat up all night,
But could only rhyme "orange" with "orange".

A young man who hailed from Crouch End,
Was easy as pie to offend,
He'd yell, stamp and cry,
And scream at the sky,
If somebody called him their friend.

A lady incredibly strong,
Knew it wouldn't be long,
Until her son, Dean,
Said something mean,
And things would go terribly wrong.

If I Were a Rich Man

If I were a rich man,
That's how the lyrics go,
And I think that should be the start and end.
I don't think I would worry,
How to biddy-biddy-bum,
On that I never, ever, could depend.

It would really be the best,
To have a load of cash,
And live a life that matches all my dreams.
But life, the way it goes,
Is toil and strain and stress,
And riches are for others, so it seems.

More Limericks

A unique young lad from BC,
Became best friends with a tree,
The conversations were short,
They spent time deep in thought,
And that, for them, was the key.

A President called Donald Trump,
Came on the scene with a thump,
His foes cried, "Impeach!",
But could only screech,
And came down to earth with a bump.

A comic book geek named Dan,
Believed that he was Superman,
But 'twas not Kryptonite,
That stole all his might,
'Twas trying to open a can.

A lady of science named Bridget,
Was a terrible fidget
She couldn't sit still,
Which made you feel ill,
While examining the latest widget.

A young French boy from Verdun,
Thought that it was really fun,
To sit in his class,
And as the teacher walked past,
Sing, "House of the Rising Sun.

When the Wind Blows

I really like it best,
When the wind is in the West,
And I also like it when it's in the East.
Praise is in my mouth,
When it's blowing from the South,
But from the North it really is a beast.

But I really never mind,
Because I always find,
That whether you are man or you are mouse,
That the North wind you can beat,
With clothing and some heat,
Staying safe and snug within your house.

Spelling Confused

In yore confusing "your" and "you're" was always frowned upon.
And mixing "there"and "their" and "they're" was never ever done.

#Trending

Praise to the one who invented the #trend,
That means #simplewords can spiral,
Out of #control and #goroundtheglobe,
And become #truly viral.

If you #hashtag #hashtag, and #othersdotoo,
#Youllneverknow #whatyoustarted,
Or what #initswake your #hashtag #mayshake,
#liketheseasbeingparted.

Homophonically Speaking

See the sea, be fine with a fine,
Or we'll get a weal from a wheel.
In the morn we'll mourn the mine that is mine,
Sounding a peal whilst we peel.
Be as a bee so that you sew,
A seam that will orderly seem.
And deliver a blow to the man who will blow,
A tune as we dance a real reel.

Yet More Limericks

A radical young lad from Louth,
Went to live in the South,
But as he expected,
He was rejected,
Because of his bad potty mouth.

An ambitious, respected old vicar,
Built his church out of whicker,
But danger there came,
From a candle flame,
And the building it burned that much quicker.

A vicious pirate cutthroat,
Thought of building a boat,
He thought it quite neat,
To use concrete,
And was shocked when it didn't float.

A lady who managed a bank,
Drove to work in a tank,
And any place,
Was her parking space,
But her popularity shrank.

A Baker who baked the best bread,
Baked a loaf that came out bright red,
He said, "This is weird",
And, "Just as I feared!"
And retired in distress to his bed.

A Facebook user named mike,
Posted a pic of his bike,
He thought it the best,
Put his belief to the test,
But he received just one like.

Lord Adonis (Who Are You?)

Hail to Lord Adonis, please tell me who you are,
Have you ever won the FA Cup,
Or raced a racing car?
Did you ever break a record, or make a work of art,
Or take on an unjust regime,
And upset their apple cart?

Were you great in public office, did you start a charity?
I must say that until Brexit,
You were unknown to me.
Did you start a massive business, and bring in loads of jobs,
Or start a street youth program,
To change the lives of yobs?

I think I know the answer, I've seen the Honours trends,
It's scratching the right backs,
And having the right friends.
Titles given to failures, to donkeys and to Dobbins,
If you want a prime example,
Just look at Olly Robbins

The "Honours" system is a joke, it's how you play the game,
It's your connections and post code,
That adds "Noble" to your name.
Find a case to change my mind, you'll be looking near and far,
Please, please, Lord Adonis,
Tell me who you are.

<u>Grave Mistake</u>

An undertaker, name of Jake made a very grave mistake,
It occured when, in a hurry, he went and buried Mrs Murray,
In the tomb of Mr Kern, whose corpse, then, he in turn,
Placed in the grave of Dev Patel, whose body was then buried, well,
In the grave of Mrs Knight, Jake then had to put this right.

He thought for hours, careless Jake, about what action he could take,
He was kind, and he was grieved about distress to the bereaved,
And so in the dark he went down and opened graves and switch
them round,
But now the twist in Jake's sad tale, for grave robbing, ten years in
jail.

And, Limericks Again

A brave young girl had a vision,
To become a great politician,
But things took a change,
And she found it quite strange,
When she ended up working in fishing.

The comic book crook, Dr Doom,
Refused to tidy his room,
His mum said, "Lad,
You may be bad,
But you'll learn to handle a broom!"

The Viking, Erik the Red,
Wore his horned helmet in bed,
Which upset his wife,
Caused marital strife,
And now he sleeps in the shed.

A man who grew lots of trees,
Tried to use wood to make cheese.
Though told dairy was missing,
He wouldn't listen,
And instead he used liquidised fleas.

A middle-aged gent named Dave,
Wanted to go to a rave,
But his mid-life crisis,
Meant paying high prices,
And took him too soon to his grave.

A lady we'll call Lucy Wood,

Thought it was terribly good,
To tip sleeping cows,
It's how she got her wows,
Her friends never quite understood.

Haiku Time

Taste in Music

I like classic rock,
And heavy metal music, too,
I have the best taste.

Waking

Early morning sun,
Greeting me as I wake refreshed,
I drink my coffee.

Children

My daughters bless me,
I witnessed them enter the world,
They are part of me.

My Wife

My wife is a joy,
She encourages me when weak,
She and I are one.

Time

Darkness rules the night,
But the light will come with daybreak,
The world is made new.

Presidential Acrostic

Defying convention
Owning his opponents
Never backs down
Always wins
Loves his country
Democrats wince

True to his promises
Rocks every boat
USA, USA, USA
Married to Melania
President.

See

See an acorn,
See an Oak,
See a ship of old, billowing sails,
See adventurers,
See lands being found,
See an acorn,
See all this.

See a seed,
See a sunflower,
See a painter, making art,
See the colours,
See delight,
See a seed,
See much more

See a child,
See the world,
See success, a life well lived,
See a land,
A place of peace,
See a child,
See what will be.

And... LIMERICKS!

A Norwegian chappy named Leif,
Became a gentleman thief,
So gallant his soul,
That nothing he stole,
And ended his time in great grief.

The world's most awful cook,
Wrote a recipe book,
There were too many germs,
In his roasted worms,
But it was very good for a rook.

A rugby song singer from Bude,
Sang songs that were terribly rude,
On long distance runs,
He sang songs to nuns,
And their thoughts became really quite lewd.

A man who encountered a ghost,
Thought it worthy of toast,
That he was believed,
And rather relieved,
That it wasn't a hollow boast.

A porter who held college keys,
Tried filling the college with bees,
He thought it quite funny,
That the students had honey,
All the way up to their knees.

Shakin' Shakespeare

Shakin' Shakespeare had a goal,
'Twasn't plays, perchance,
But to invent, Rock n' Roll,
For folk to jump and prance.
Oh, 'tis true, he had a quiff,
He was the early king,
But the nation was too stiff,
For this brand new "thing".

Shakin' Shakespeare wanted Jive,
They, the old Gavotte,
He wanted music loud and live,
They, sadly, did not.
"Daddy-O!" the young bard cried,
"Please don't be so square."
Shakin' Shakespeare couldn't hide,
His hipster-like despair.

Shakin' Shakespeare tried for years,
To make England cool,
However, to the people's ears,
He seemed more and more the fool.
He resigned himself to write for stage,
Accepting of the facts,
It would await another age,
To be cool for cats.

Printed in Great Britain
by Amazon

35448002R00021